Everybody Loves Bentley

A Puppy's Quest to Find Love and Happiness

by

RaNae D. Clark

DORRANCE
PUBLISHING CO
EST. 1920
PITTSBURGH, PENNSYLVANIA 15238

Dorrance Publishing Co
585 Alpha Drive
Pittsburgh, PA 15238
Visit our website at www.dorrancebookstore.com

ISBN: 979-8-8860-4355-6
eISBN: 979-8-8860-4451-5

Hi, my name is Bentley, Jr. What is your name?

I was born in Nome, Alaska, on December 2nd. If you don't know anything about Alaska, it is very cold in the winter, colder than you can imagine. Where were you born and when is your birthday?

I do not remember my Mom or Dad, but I do remember being all alone and searching for food because I was so hungry. I roamed the freezing streets of Nome from morning until night, when I was too tired to walk any further. I would look for the warmest spot to lie down, trying to find a place away from the snow. I begged for food and ate anything that smelled like food. And yes, sometimes I went to sleep hungry. Have you ever gone to bed hungry?

When I was almost three months old, I was picked up by Animal Control and taken to a place called the pound. Have you ever been to the pound? Have you ever adopted a pet?

It was warm, and I was given lots of food, so I thought I had it pretty good. I decided right then that I would eat any kind of food anyone offered me. I would not even smell it. One day, a family came to the pound and adopted me. I could tell right off they were not the kind of family I wanted to live with. When I got to their house, I saw they had two cats so I chased them all over the house. That did not make the family very happy, so they returned me to the pound the very next day. They said I did not fit in with their family. I thought there must be a better family who would want to adopt and love me.

A couple who lived in Rifle, Colorado, visited their son Christian in Nome and fell in love with his dog. His name was Bentley. The couple told their son that if he ever saw a dog just like his dog, to let them know. Bentley was kind of funny looking, but he was so much fun to play with. Whenever he rolled on his back and was tickled on his stomach, he would growl like he was really mad and was going to bite, but he never did. Bentley also loved to play with dog toys and would growl a lot. He especially loved to play tug of war. Growling was just the way he played, but it made everyone laugh.

Christian called his parents one day to tell them there was a puppy at the pound that looked just like his Bentley. THAT WAS ME! The couple asked Christian what the puppy looked like, so he sent them a picture. The picture was just of my head. His parents wanted to know what the rest of me looked like and Christian laughed and said, "Funny." They said they definitely wanted to adopt me. His parents were so excited. I think they loved me already. What do you think?

The next day Christian called to tell his parents that I had already been adopted by someone else. His parents were very sad. The following day someone from the pound called Christian and told him I was returned to the pound and asked if he thought his parents still wanted to adopt me. He called his parents and told them the good news. They told Christian they definitely wanted to adopt me and said they would make travel arrangements to have me flown to Denver, Colorado, where they would pick me up.

Christian went to the pound to pick me up, but the pound was closed.
I did not know what was going to happen to me, but at least I had food
and water, so I was patient while I waited for my new family. Christian
was about to drive home when a policeman stopped him and asked if
he needed to get in the pound, that he had a key. The nice policeman
let Christian in the pound and he picked me up. I was really happy because he seemed very nice and maybe he wanted to adopt me. Have
you ever met a nice policeman?

After I spent the night at Christian's house, he drove me to a big, noisy place called an airport. I was put in a dog crate and waited and waited and waited. Then I was put in a big, noisy thing called an airplane and flown from Nome to Anchorage, Alaska. Have you ever been in an airplane? If you have been in an airplane, do you remember how noisy it is?

Finally, I was taken off the airplane and put on another airplane and was flown from Anchorage to Seattle, Washington. Much later, I was taken off that airplane and put on another airplane and flown from Seattle to Denver, Colorado. The airplane was very loud and vibrated but the sound just put me sleep. The airplane was an hour late getting to Denver, but Christian's parents waited anxiously for my arrival. I was excited because I just knew I was on my way to my new family.

The whole time I was traveling, I was a good boy and did not have an accident in my crate. Can you believe it, I was on an airplane for thirteen hours? I sure wanted the family to like me. When I finally arrived and the family opened my crate, the woman said, "Oh, he is so cute." I was the happiest puppy in the whole wide world. I could tell that they loved me at first sight! They were my new mom and dad.

My new mom and dad put me in a nice, warm bed in the center of their truck for a three-hour drive to my new home in Rifle. They petted me often and offered me food and water. While my dad was busy driving their truck, my mom kept kissing and hugging me. They decided right then they would name me Bentley, just like the dog their son had. They said I looked so much like Christian's Bentley. I was so happy I could hardly stand it. When was the happiest time in your life?

It took me awhile to realize there was another dog in the back seat of the truck. I learned her name was Cheyenne. She was a beautiful small Australian Shepard and looked very kind. Do you have a dog?

There was a snowstorm while we were driving home, but that did not bother me because I was used to snowstorms in Nome. About halfway home it began to rain, and something started going back and forth very fast on the front window. I did not know what they were but my mom said they were just windshield wipers. I had never seen windshield wipers before, so every time they started moving back and forth, I barked at them. My new family thought that was pretty funny, so I knew I was off to a good start. Maybe they would not return me to the pound. Maybe I finally found my forever home. Maybe they loved me.

My mom and dad lived on a forty-acre ranch and had two cats and two horses. When I went into their ranch house, I was greeted by two cats. Do you have a cat?

The cats and I smelled each other and then they got bored and just walked away. I did not want to chase them because I was so happy and I did not want to be taken to the pound again. I had never seen horses before so I was really excited to visit them. Do you like horses?

A few weeks later I noticed there were about six horses down
the lane from where we lived, so I walked down to visit them.
Suddenly, my mom and dad noticed I was not around and were
calling and calling, "Bentley, Bentley, Bentley." I was not quite
used to my name being Bentley, so I did not pay any attention.
My mom and dad did not know where I had taken off to. After
a while, my mom noticed I was way down the lane walking around
the horse's long legs. They were huge. My mom was afraid for
me because I was so small. She ran down the lane and immediately
picked me up and took me home. She did not even scold me. Do
you have a horse?

Life on a ranch was so fun. Lots of exploring and seeing different types of animals I had never seen before, like elk, deer, and lots of bunnies. Have you seen any of these animals?

I quickly became friends with Cheyenne and we would chase each other and play all the time. After it snowed, we would jump and play in the snow. I could tell Cheyenne loved me. Life was good. My mom and dad could tell Cheyenne and I were very happy living on our ranch, so they decided to name our road "Happy Dog Trail." My mom and dad took Cheyenne and me traveling to Yellowstone National Park in Wyoming one year and Glacier National Park in Montana the next year. Have you ever been to Yellowstone or Glacier National Park?

When we went to Glacier National Park the second time, my
mom and dad fell in love with a seven-week old chihuahua.
They named her Shelby because we had driven through the town of
Shelby, Montana, and they liked the name Shelby. Neither Cheyenne
nor I was very interested in Shelby because she was so small
and we did not want to hurt her. She always wanted to be held.
Cheyenne and I were kind of jealous. Have you ever been jealous?

One night my mom and dad watched a movie they thought would be fun to watch. It was called "Hatchi." It was based on a true story about a dog that always walked with his dad to the train station so his dad could go to work. The dog would always come back to the train station right before the train stopped to let his dad off coming home from work. He did this every single day for years and years. I was sitting on my mom's lap and actually watched the entire movie. I was so tired toward the end of the movie I was watching it with my head down. I love to watch television when there is any kind of animal on it because I run up and either bark at it or whine.

We lived in Rifle for five years before moving to Arizona. We had a big trailer camper and lived in it for seven months while we looked for a new home to buy. Fortunately, there was a dog park where I got to meet other dogs and a lot of fun people. Cheyenne would chase a tennis ball whenever anyone would throw it for her. I just wanted to look around, smell other dogs, and jump up on people's laps. I knew everyone loved me, so I knew no one would mind. Shelby made friends with another chihuahua named Becca Sue. They were just like sisters. Do you have a sister?

We also got to go for walks and visit family. That was really fun,
especially when we visited Grandma because she would share
her dog's food with us. She always had roast or chicken, cooked
carrots, cottage cheese, and pasta. She made food for her dog,
who was a shih-tzu named Josh. And, she also fed our cousin's dog,
named Kandi. Grandma loved to hand little pieces of food
to us, one at a time. I could tell she loved us. I always jumped up
on her lap every time she sat down. It always surprised her. We also
liked to go to my uncle's house because he would feed us steak.
I could tell he loved me too. Do you like steak?

We finally found a house in New River, Arizona, and that is
where I currently live. Cheyenne and I can smell coyotes from
inside our house, and as soon as we do, we start barking to warn
our mom and dad. And, sometimes, when we are outside, we
can see them through our fence. We bark like crazy because we
do not want them in our yard. Cheyenne and I know one of our
jobs are to protect our property and little Shelby. There are lots
of bunnies too and I love to chase them. Have you ever seen a
coyote?

Sometimes I think back to when I was just a puppy and had to find food for myself and a place to sleep. It seemed like no one wanted to help me. I felt like no one would ever love me. Well, look at me now! I am the happiest dog in the whole wide world because everyone loves me!

Something happened recently. Christian came to our house
for a visit and we were all talking about how much I was like
his Bentley. Their son told them he found out that I came
from the same home as his Bentley. That is when they knew
I must be his Bentley's son. So, they all decided to name me
Bentley, Jr.

This is the end of my story for now, now that I know everybody
loves me!

You can use these blank pages to write about your favorite animals and pets.

Printed in the USA
CPSIA information can be obtained
at www.ICGtesting.com
LVHW070531140823
755121LV00006B/144